Just Joking

NATIONAL GEOGRAPHIC KiDS

300
hilarious jokes, tricky tongue twisters, and ridiculous riddles

NATIONAL GEOGRAPHIC
WASHINGTON, D.C.

Lions rest for about
20 hours a day.

4

A sea otter's fur helps it float by trapping air inside the strands.

KNOCK, KNOCK.

Who's there?
Lena.
Lena who?
Lena little closer and I'll tell you.

TONGUE TWISTER!

Say this fast three times:

Rolling red wagons race wildly down roads.

Q How are **two banana peels** like shoes?

A They're a pair of slippers.

7

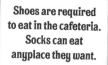

Shoes are required
to eat in the cafeteria.
Socks can eat
anyplace they want.

Q What do you call a shy lamb?

A Baaash-ful.

Q Why did cavemen draw pictures of hippopotamuses and rhinoceroses on their wall?

A Because they couldn't spell the animals' names.

Q

On what
nuts
can
pictures
hang?

Wall-nuts.

8

A Reinwardt's flying frog has webbed feet to help it glide down from the treetops.

KNOCK, KNOCK.

Who's there?
Ewan.
Ewan who?
It's just me.

9

Grizzly bears can run up to 30 miles an hour (48 kph).

Q What happened when 500 hares got loose in the center of town?

A The police had to comb the area.

Q What do you call a very popular perfume?

A A best-smeller.

HA! HA! HA! HA! HA! HA! HA! HA! HA! HA! HA! HA!

The American alligator species is more than 150 million years old.

KNOCK, KNOCK.

Who's there?
Nuisance.
Nuisance who?
What's nuisance yesterday?

13

A polar bear has rough paw pads to keep it from slipping on the ice.

What do you call a polar bear wearing earmuffs?

Anything you want. He can't hear you!

Say this fast three times:

Dracula digs dreary, dark dungeons.

Q What happens when a ghost gets lost in the fog?

A He is mist.

Q What do you call two spiders that just got married?

A Newlywebs.

Q What paces back and forth on the ocean floor?

A A nervous wreck.

15

Cooks cook cup

cakes quickly.

A female lion usually gives birth to three to five lion cubs at a time.

KNOCK, KNOCK.

Who's there?
Cash.
Cash who?
No, thanks. I prefer peanuts.

18

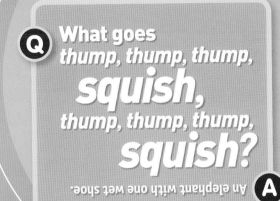

Q **What goes** *thump, thump, thump,* **squish,** *thump, thump, thump,* **squish?**

A An elephant with one wet shoe.

TONGUE TWISTER!

Say this fast three times:

Jolly juggling jesters juggle jingle jacks.

19

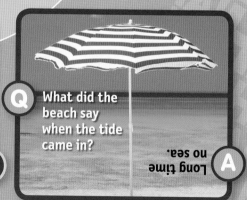

TONGUE TWISTER!

Say this fast three times:

Nat the bat ate Pat the gnat.

Q What kind of fish goes best with peanut butter?

A Jellyfish.

Q When is a baseball player like a spider?

A When he catches a fly.

Q What did the beach say when the tide came in?

A Long time no sea.

20

KNOCK, KNOCK.

Who's there?
Hugo
Hugo who?
Hugo-ing to let me in or not?

About 99 percent of a red panda's diet is bamboo.

Bulldogs can weigh as much as 50 pounds—that's more than three bowling balls.

24

Q What did the chewing gum say to the shoe?

A I'm stuck on you.

Q What goes **zzub zzub?**

A A bee flying backward.

TONGUE TWISTER!

Say this fast three times:

Quick kiss, quicker kiss.

Q What is in an astronaut's favorite sandwich?

A Launch meat.

25

CUSTOMER:
Do you serve
crabs?

WAITRESS:
Of course, sir.
We serve
anyone.

Q **Did you just pick your nose?**

A No. I've had it since I was born.

Q What has a big **mouth** and doesn't say a word?

A A river.

Q Why does it get hot after a baseball game?

A Because all the fans have left.

26

Fishers are mammals found only in northern North America.

KNOCK, KNOCK.

Who's there?
Ben.
Ben who?
Ben knocking on the door all afternoon.

27

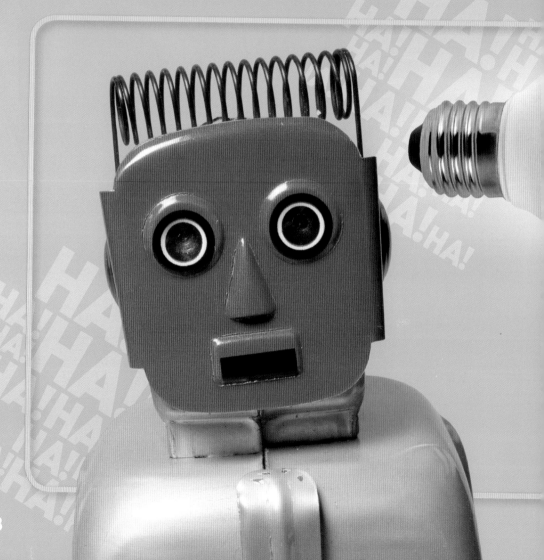

HA! HA! HA! HA! HA! HA! HA! HA! HA! HA!

Why did the robot eat a lightbulb?

Because he was in need of a light snack.

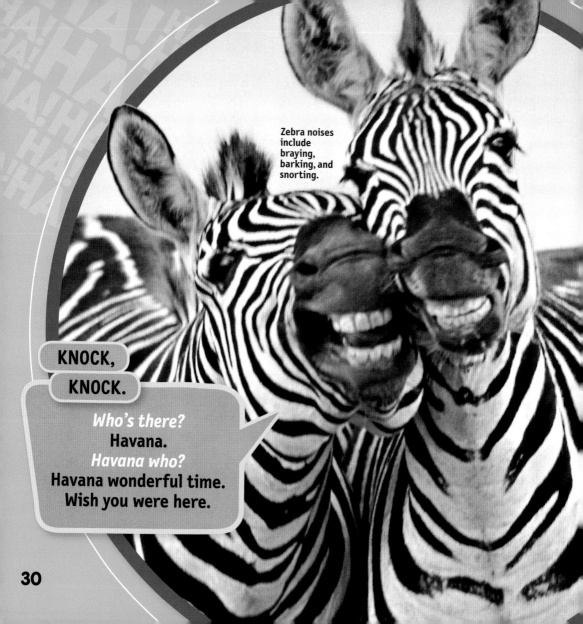

Zebra noises include braying, barking, and snorting.

KNOCK, KNOCK.

Who's there?
Havana.
Havana who?
Havana wonderful time. Wish you were here.

Q What do **planets** use to download **music?**

A Neptunes.

Q Why does Santa have three gardens?

A So he can hoe, hoe, hoe!

31

Q Why are grapes never alone?

A Because they hang out in a bunch.

Q How do **bees** get to **school**?

A On the school buzz.

TONGUE TWISTER!

Say this fast three times:

A moose noshes much mush.

Q What do you call a **COW** that doesn't give milk?

A A milk dud.

KNOCK, KNOCK.

Who's there?
Olive.
Olive who?
Olive you!

The word "hamster" comes from the German word *hamstern*, meaning to hoard.

33

The Roseate spoonbill's wingspan is more than four feet (1.2 m) wide.

What protects a
clown
from the sun?

The bozone layer.

Q What did the **Atlantic Ocean** say to the **Pacific Ocean?**

A Nothing. It just waved.

TONGUE TWISTER!

Say this fast three times:

Comical cactus curls rural wind.

Q What do anteaters have that other animals don't have?

A Baby anteaters.

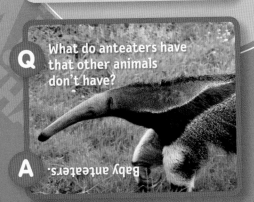

Q What did one **math book** say to the other math book?

A I've got a lot of problems.

Q What happened to the frog that parked illegally?

A He was toad away.

Q What asks no questions but must be answered?

A The doorbell.

HA! HA! HA! HA! HA! HA! HA! HA! HA! HA! HA! HA! HA!

A baby orca, or calf, is usually born tail-first.

KNOCK, KNOCK.

Who's there?
Adair.
Adair who?
Adair once, but now
I'm bald.

39

Patty picks pretty

paper packages.

What two things can you **not** have for breakfast?

Lunch and dinner.

Q What do planets **read?**

A Comet books.

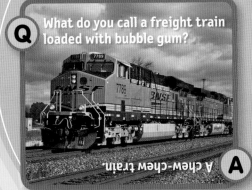

Q What do you call a freight train loaded with bubble gum?

A A chew-chew train.

DOCTOR: You need new glasses.

PATIENT: How do you know? I haven't told you what's wrong with me yet.

DOCTOR: I could tell as soon as you walked in through the window.

43

Arctic ground squirrels hibernate seven months out of the year.

KNOCK, KNOCK.

Who's there?
Huron.
Huron who?
Huron my toe. Could you please get off it?

TONGUE TWISTER!

Say this fast three times:

An ape hates grapes.

Q What has **two legs** but can't walk?

A A pair of pants.

46

There are 17 species
of macaws, including this
military macaw.

TONGUE TWISTER!

Say this fast three times:

A tiny tiger thinks tough thoughts.

Q What do cows and dogs have in common?

A They both like classical music, Moo-zart and Wag-ner.

Q How do you turn **soup** into **gold?**

A Add 24 carrots.

Q If chickens wake up when the rooster crows, when do ducks wake up?

A At the quack of dawn.

Why did **Dracula** become a **vegetarian?**

Because his doctor told him "stake" was bad for his heart.

Sea otters use their stomachs as tables while they snack.

KNOCK, KNOCK.

Who's there?
Annie.
Annie who?
Annie body home?

50

Q Why did the **cat** put an **M** into the **freezer?**

A It turns into mice.

TONGUE TWISTER!

Say this fast three times:

Brenda's bunny baked buttered bread.

Q Why did the chicken cross the dusty road twice?

A Because she was a dirty double-crosser.

Q What do you call a nervous zucchini?

A An edgy veggie.

Like most parrots, Budgerigar parakeets have two toes facing forward and two facing back.

What do you get when you cross a **parakeet** with a lawn mower**?**

Shredded tweet!

African lions live in groups called prides.

KNOCK, KNOCK.

Who's there?
Kenya.
Kenya who?
Kenya guess who it is?

Say this fast three times:

Speak sphinx.

Q How is baseball like cake?

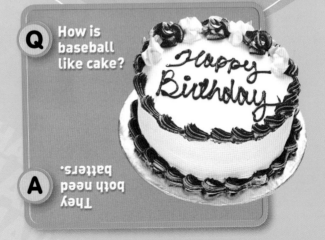

A They both need batters.

55

MOTHER: Jay, let your brother have the sled half the time!

JAY: I do, Mom. I have it going downhill and he has it going up.

Q

What do George **Washington,** Christopher **Columbus,** and Abraham **Lincoln** have in common?

A They were all born on a holiday!

Q

What can hold a **car** but can't lift a feather?

A A garage.

Q How do baby birds learn how to fly?

A They wing it.

TOURIST: How would you describe the **rain** in this part of the country?

LOCAL: Little drops of water falling from the sky.

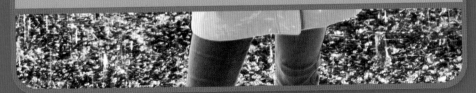

KNOCK, KNOCK.

Who's there?
Distressing.
Distressing who?
Distressing has too much vinegar!

A crocodile's eyes and nostrils are on top of its head so it can see and breathe when lying just below the water's surface.

KNOCK, KNOCK.

Who's there?
Scold.
Scold who?
Scold out here!

Gentoo penguins are the fastest diving birds in the world.

Q

What travels around the world but never leaves its corner?

A
A postage stamp.

TONGUE TWISTER!

Say this fast three times:

Many an anemone sees an enemy anemone.

Q
What do you get when you cross a **turkey** with a **centipede?**

A
Drumsticks for everyone.

Q
Why are dolphins more clever than humans?

A
Dolphins can train people to feed them fish.

Q What is the best way to keep dogs out of the street?

A Put them in a barking lot.

TONGUE TWISTER!

Say this fast three times:

Sly Sam slurps Sally's soup.

Tegus are large carnivorous lizards that grow up to 4 feet long (1.2 m).

KNOCK, KNOCK.

Who's there?
Woo.
Woo who?
Don't get so excited—
it's just a joke.

63

What do you call a **cat** that **bowls?**

An alley cat.

Roughly 30 percent of households in the United States own at least one cat.

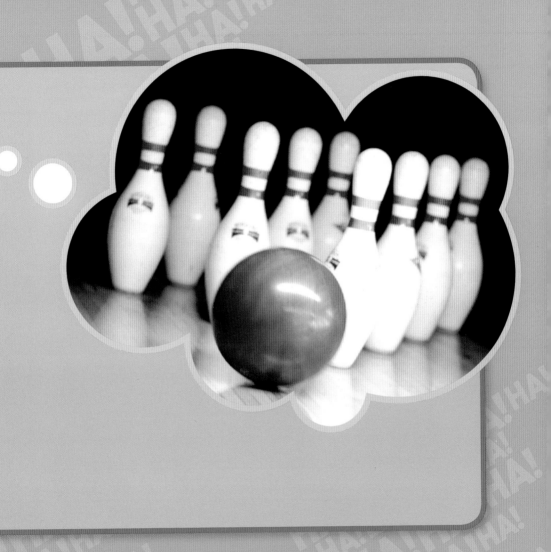

Elephant seals live in both extremely cold and extremely warm places, including Antarctica and Mexico.

TONGUE TWISTER!

Say this fast three times:

See Shep slip.

Q What do you get when you cross a bear with a skunk?

A Winnie the phew.

67

Say this fast three times:

Are our oars oak?

Q What is a monster's favorite place to swim?

A Lake Erie.

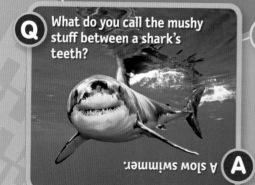

Q What do you call the mushy stuff between a shark's teeth?

A A slow swimmer.

Q How does a mouse feel after a bath?

A Squeaky clean.

68

Where do smart **hot dogs** end up?

On the honor roll.

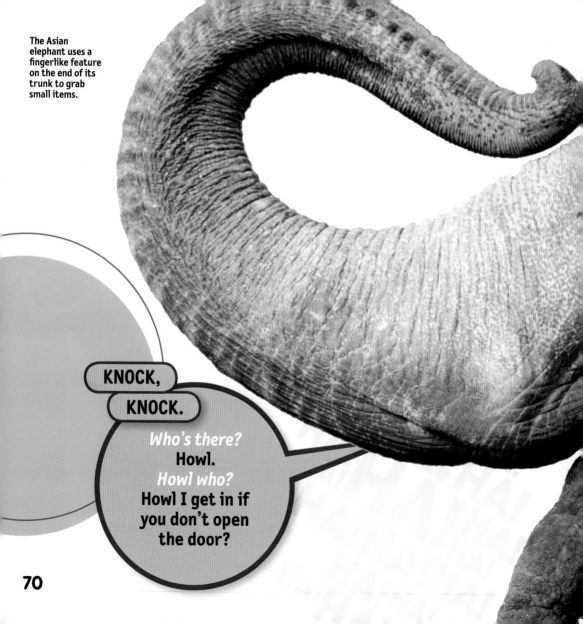

The Asian elephant uses a fingerlike feature on the end of its trunk to grab small items.

KNOCK, KNOCK.

Who's there?
Howl.
Howl who?
Howl I get in if you don't open the door?

KNOCK, KNOCK.

Who's there?
Waddle.
Waddle who?
Waddle I do if you don't open the door?

Like all ducks, this Pekin duck's feet have no blood vessels or nerves, so its feet never get cold.

Q Why did the farmer plow his field with a steamroller?

A Because he wanted mashed potatoes.

Q What do you get when you **cross a pig** with a **centipede?**

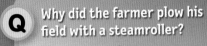

A Bacon and legs.

TONGUE TWISTER!

Say this fast three times:

Susie sailed the seven seas.

73

Q How do you communicate with a fish?

A Drop it a line.

Q What nails do carpenters hate to hit?

A Fingernails.

TONGUE TWISTER!

Say this fast three times:

Which wristwatch is a Swiss wristwatch?

Q What did the cheeseburger name its daughter?

A Patty.

74

TONGUE TWISTER!

Say this fast three times:

Ten tricky two-toed turkeys trotted.

She freed

six sheep.

Sheep travel in flocks to protect themselves from predators.

A serval can leap ten feet in the air and change direction mid-leap.

KNOCK, KNOCK.

Who's there?
Cook.
Cook who?
Hey! Who are you calling a cuckoo?

Q Why did the crook take a bath before he robbed the bank?

A So he could make a clean getaway.

TONGUE TWISTER!

Say this fast three times:

She shouldn't shake the salt shakers, should she?

TEACHER: Why does the Statue of Liberty stand in New York harbor?

STUDENT: Because it can't sit down.

Q How do you fix a broken jack-o'-lantern?

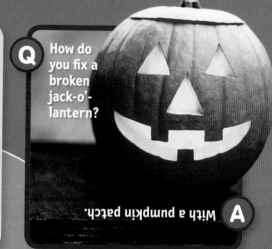

A With a pumpkin patch.

Q What is at the **end** of everything?

A The letter g.

TONGUE TWISTER!

Say this fast three times:

6 silly sisters sort short socks.

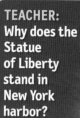

Bare-backed fruit bats live in Australia, Indonesia, Papua New Guinea, and East Timor.

81

Dromedary camels have one hump; Bactrian camels, like this one, have two.

A green tree frog's call sounds like "quonk, quonk, quonk."

KNOCK, KNOCK.

Who's there?
Twig.
Twig who?
Twig or treat!

Q What has a **bottom** at the top?

A Your legs!

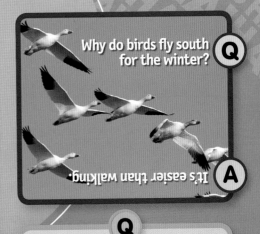

Q Why do birds fly south for the winter?

A It's easier than walking.

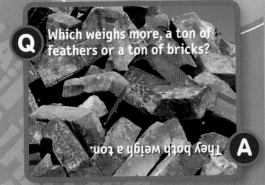

Q Which weighs more, a ton of feathers or a ton of bricks?

A They both weigh a ton.

Q What did one **ghost** say to the other ghost?

A "Get a life!"

Q

How do fleas travel from place to place?

A

They itch-hike.

Q When do you go at red and stop at green?

A When you're eating watermelon.

HA!HA!HA!HA!HA!HA!HA!HA!HA!HA!

This Asian elephant has smaller, rounder ears than an African elephant.

HA! HA! HA! HA! HA! HA! HA! HA!

KNOCK, KNOCK.

Who's there?
Figs.
Figs who?
Figs the doorbell—
it's broken!

87

What would you get if you crossed a jazz musician with a sweet potato?

Yam sessions.

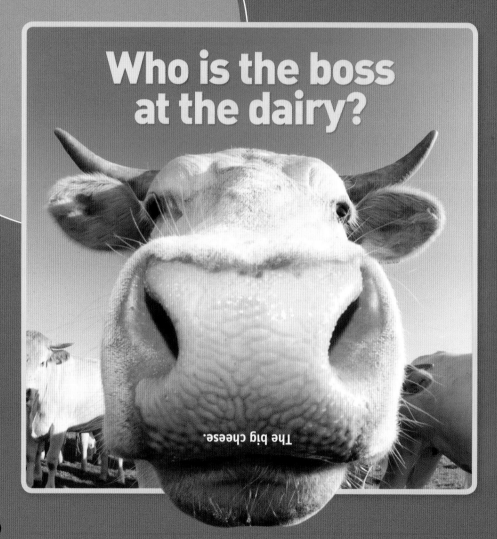

Who is the boss at the dairy?

The big cheese.

Q What did the
digital watch
say to the
grandfather
clock?

A "Look, Grandpa, no hands."

Q What did the blanket
say to the bed?

A "Got you covered."

Q What do
you say
when you
meet a
two-
headed
monster?

A "Hello, hello."

Q A man rode into
town on Friday,
stayed for 5 days,
and then rode
home on Friday.
How is this possible?

A His horse was named Friday.

Q What do you call an elephant at the North Pole?

A Lost.

Q Who makes a living while driving **customers** away?

A A taxi driver.

Q What do cats like to eat for breakfast?

A Mice crispies.

What do you get when you cross a snowman with a shark?

Frostbite.

93

KNOCK, KNOCK.

Who's there?
Nadia.
Nadia who?
Nadia head if you understand what I'm saying.

What country

did candy come from?

Sweeten.

A bearded dragon's "beard" is a spike-filled throat pouch that it puffs out for protection.

KNOCK, KNOCK.

Who's there?
Walrus.
Walrus who?
Why do you walrus ask that silly question?

Q What did the duck say to the bunny?

A "You quack me up!"

Q What do you call it when **crooks** go surfing?

A A crime wave.

99

Q Why did the **baby cookie** cry?

A Because its mother was a wafer so long.

TONGUE TWISTER!

Say this fast three times:

Girl gargoyle, guy gargoyle.

Two snakes are talking.
SNAKE 1: "Are we venomous?"
SNAKE 2: "Yes, why?"
SNAKE 1: "I just bit my lip."

Q If the dictionary goes from **A** to **Z**, what goes from **Z** to **A**?

A A zebra.

KNOCK, KNOCK.

Who's there?
Little old lady.
Little old lady who?
Hey, why are you yodeling?

This African leopard's spots, called rosettes, help it blend into its surroundings.

What did the
window
say to the
door?

"What are you squeaking about?
I'm the one with the panes!"

This tropical rainbow toucan sleeps by folding its tail over its head and resting its long bill over its back.

JULIE: What's the difference between a chimp and a pizza?

JOHN: I don't know.

JULIE: Remind me not to send you to the grocery store!

Q What kind of **bird** can **write?**

A A penguin.

Q How do you close an **envelope** underwater?

A With a seal.

Q Why did the guy put a stove in his car?

A To make a hot rod.

Q What did the hat say to the scarf?

A You go around while I go on ahead.

Q What do you get when you cross a **fish** with an **elephant?**

A Swimming trunks.

Q How do you warm up a **room** after it's been **painted?**

A Give it a second coat.

CUSTOMER: "There's a dead beetle in my soup."

WAITER: "Yes, sir, they're not very good swimmers."

What happens when you tell an egg a **joke?**

It cracks up.

Tigers have been known to eat up to 60 pounds (27 kg) of meat in one night.

KNOCK, KNOCK.

Who's there?
Alaska.
Alaska who?
Alaska only one more time to open the door.

Have you ever seen a line drive? **Q**

A No, but I've seen a ballpark.

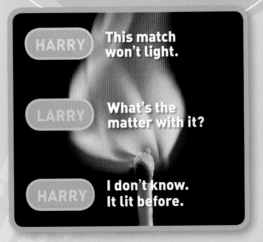

HARRY: This match won't light.

LARRY: What's the matter with it?

HARRY: I don't know. It lit before.

A pig is born with 28 baby teeth that later fall out.

KNOCK, KNOCK.

Who's there?
Dozen.
Dozen who?
Dozen anybody want to play with me?

Q What do snowmen wear on their heads?

A Ice caps.

Q Where do snowflakes dance?

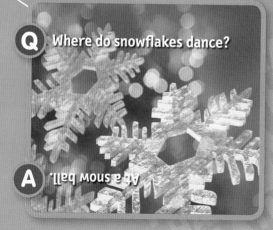

A At a snow ball.

Caribou are the only deer species in which both males and females have antlers.

KNOCK, KNOCK.

Who's there?
Luke.
Luke who?
Luke through the peephole and you'll see.

113

TONGUE TWISTER!

Say this fast three times:

Red bulb,

blue bulb.

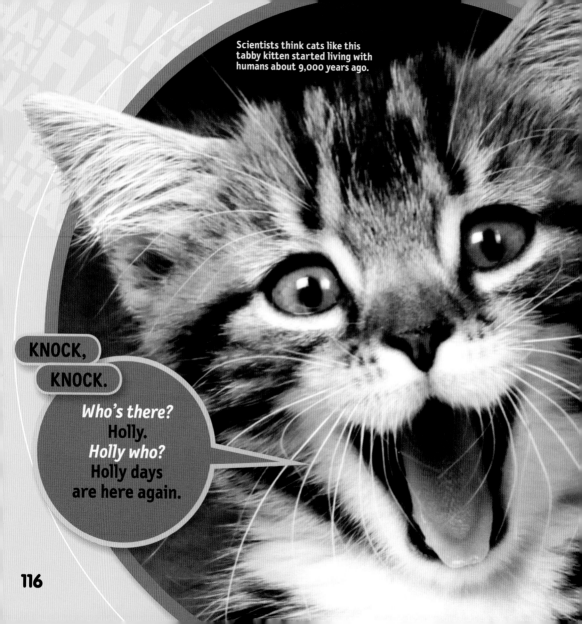

Scientists think cats like this tabby kitten started living with humans about 9,000 years ago.

KNOCK, KNOCK.

Who's there?
Holly.
Holly who?
Holly days are here again.

Say this fast three times:

Trained **turtles** trotted to the **track.**

Q Why wouldn't they let the butterfly into the dance?

A Because it was a moth ball.

117

TONGUE TWISTER!

Say this fast three times:

At eight Edgar ate eight eggs.

Q Why did the cowboy put his bunk in the fireplace?

A So he could sleep like a log.

Q Why did the farmer's wife chase the chickens out of the yard?

A They were using fowl language.

Q What do you give an elephant that's going to be sick?

A Plenty of room.

118

Why did the tomato blush?

Because it saw the salad dressing.

120

Golden mantella frogs live on the African island of Madagascar and can be yellow, orange, or red.

A Hermann's tortoise can live for up to 30 years.

KNOCK, KNOCK.

Who's there?
Gorilla.
Gorilla who?
Gorilla me a steak.

Did you hear about the long-distance runner who took part in a 50-mile race? He was in the lead and had one more mile to go, but he was too tired to finish. So he turned around and ran back!

Q How did the cow feel when it struck out every time it came to bat?

A Like an udder failure.

Q What rock group has **four men** who **don't sing?**

A Mount Rushmore.

123

Q Why did the **gum** cross the road?

A Because it was stuck on the chicken's foot.

Q How do you keep a turkey in suspense?

A I'll tell you later!

TONGUE TWISTER!

Say this fast three times:

Six smart sharks swam swiftly.

Q What did the **bee** sit on?

A Its bee-hind.

Double bubble gum bubbles double.

Why do hummingbirds hum?

Because they forgot the words.

Koalas spend as many as 18 hours a day napping or resting.

KNOCK, KNOCK.

Who's there?
Justin.
Justin who?
Justin the neighborhood.
Thought I'd stop by.

128

Q What happens when you annoy a clock?

A It gets ticked off!

TONGUE TWISTER!

Say this fast three times:

See me sneak in my squeaky, reeking sneakers.

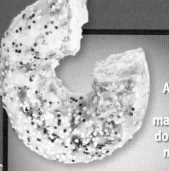

Q Why did Annie stop making dough-nuts?

A She got bored with the hole business.

Q What did the baseball glove say to the baseball?

A Catch you later.

TONGUE TWISTER!

Say this fast three times:

Two twins twirled twelve tires.

KNOCK, KNOCK.

Who's there?
T-rex.
T-rex who?
There's a T-rex at your door and you want to know its name?

Squirrel monkeys live in groups of up to 100 members.

Most geckos have transparent eyelids that they keep clean with their tongues.

KNOCK, KNOCK.

Who's there?
Phillip.
Phillip who?
Phillip my bag with treats, please.

Say this fast three times:

If a black bug bleeds black blood, what color blood does a blue bug bleed?

Q Why couldn't the teddy bear eat his dessert?

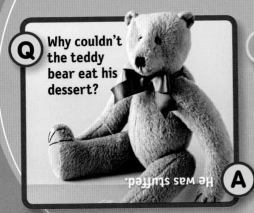

A He was stuffed.

Q What would you get if you crossed a judge with poison ivy?

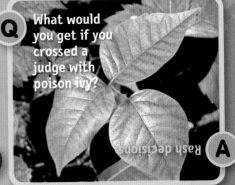

A Rash decisions

Q What did the beaver say to the log?

A "It's been nice gnawing you."

Q What is the worst thing you're likely to find in a school cafeteria?

A The food.

TONGUE TWISTER!

Say this fast three times:

Sally saw Shelley singing swimming songs.

Q

What do you call a mom or dad you can **see** through?

Transparent.

A

HA!HA!HA!HA!HA!HA!HA!HA!HA!HA!HA!

Dogs sleep 12 hours a day on average.

KNOCK,

KNOCK.

Who's there?
Tamara.
Tamara who?
Tamara we'll have leftovers!

137

I wish to wish the wish you wish to wish, but if you wish the wish the witch wishes, I won't wish the wish you wish to wish.

KNOCK, KNOCK.

Who's there?
D1.
D1 who?
D1 who knocked!

To evade predators, a puffer fish balloons up by filling its stomach with huge amounts of water.

Q Why do gorillas have big nostrils?

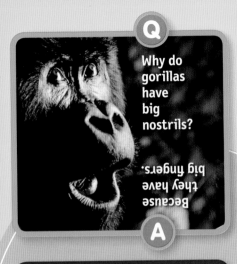

A Because they have big fingers.

Q Why are the rates at the Bird Paradise Hotel so much better than at other four-star hotels?

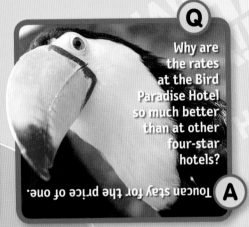

A Toucan stay for the price of one.

Q What kind of suit does a duck wear?

A A dux-edo.

Q Why did the **tonsils** get dressed up?

A Because the doctor was taking them out.

141

CUSTOMER:
Waitress, there's a fly in my soup!

WAITRESS:
Don't worry. We won't charge you extra for it.

Q Which side of the turkey is the left side?

A The part that was not eaten.

Q

Why do **soccer players** do well in school?

Because they use their heads.

A

TONGUE TWISTER!

Say this fast three times:

Two totally tired toads tripped.

How do you tell which end of a worm is its head?

You tickle the middle and see which end giggles!

A group of
mallard ducks
in flight is
called a sord.

145

While turtles live in almost any habitat, tortoises live on land.

What do you get when you cross a tortoise and a porcupine?

A porcupine's Latin name, *Erethizon dorsatum*, means "quill pig."

A slowpoke.

As many as 750 baboons, like this Hamadryas baboon, will sleep together for protection from predators.

148

TONGUE TWISTER!

Say this fast three times:

Three free thoughtful seals.

Q Why is it hard to carry on a conversation with a goat?

A They're always butting in.

149

Q Can you name the capital of all U.S. states in two seconds?

A Washington, D.C.

Q Why did the **football** coach go to the bank?

A To get his quarter back.

Q Why does the **ocean** roar?

A You'd roar too if you had crabs on your bottom.

Q Why couldn't the bicycle stand up?

A Because it was two tired.

HA!HA!HA!HA!HA!HA!

What do you call a pig with three eyes?

A piiig.

Six slick sight

seers click.

153

Only the male impalas have long, ridged horns.

KNOCK, KNOCK.

Who's there?
Boo.
Boo who?
There, there. Please don't cry.

154

Q What did the smashed banana say when an elephant sat on it?

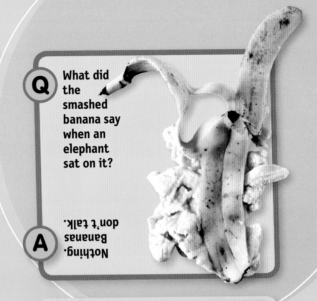

A Nothing. Bananas don't talk.

Q Why was the piano on the porch?

A Because it lost its keys.

155

Q What do you call a grizzly bear with no teeth?

A A gummy bear.

Q What do you do if a **teacher** rolls her eyes at you?

A Pick them up and roll them back to her.

Q What takes **dentists** on short trips?

A The tooth ferry.

Q What did one broom say to the other broom?

A "Have you heard the latest dirt?"

The Arabian stallion is one of the world's oldest breeds of riding horse.

KNOCK, KNOCK.

Who's there?
Amos.
Amos who?
A mosquito bit me.

157

KNOCK, KNOCK.

Who's there?
Frank.
Frank who?
Frank you for being my friend.

The African penguin makes a donkeylike braying sound.

158

Why did the **spider** cross the road?

To get to the other Web site.

Q What do you call a rabbit that is owned by a beetle?

A A bug's bunny.

Q If a runner gets athlete's foot, what does an astronaut get?

A Missile toe.

Q Why did the lion spit out the clown?

A Because he tasted funny.

Q What do you do when your **poodle** won't stop **sneezing?**

A Call a dog-tor.

Q What did the dog say when its tail got caught in the door?

A "It won't be long now."

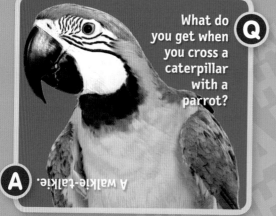

Q What do you get when you cross a caterpillar with a parrot?

A A walkie-talkie.

HA!HA!HA!HA!HA!HA!HA!HA!HA!HA!

This agamid lizard lives in Indonesia.

163

Is it hard to spot

a leopard?

No, they come that way!

Red foxes prey on small game, such as rabbits, rodents, and birds.

KNOCK,
KNOCK.

Who's there?
Auto.
Auto who?
Auto know, but I've forgotten.

166

TONGUE TWISTER!

Say this fast three times:

The ocean sure soaked Sherman.

What did the pelican say when it finished shopping? **Q**

A "Put it on my bill."

167

Donkeys are the smallest members of the horse family.

169

Q

What starts with an e, ends in an e, but only has one **letter?**

A An envelope.

Q What sports are trains good at?

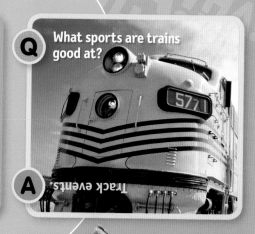

A Track events.

Q Why is basketball such a messy sport?

A Because the players dribble all over the court.

Q What has more lives than a cat?

A A frog. It croaks every night.

Did you **hear** the joke about the **roof?**

Never mind. It's over your head.

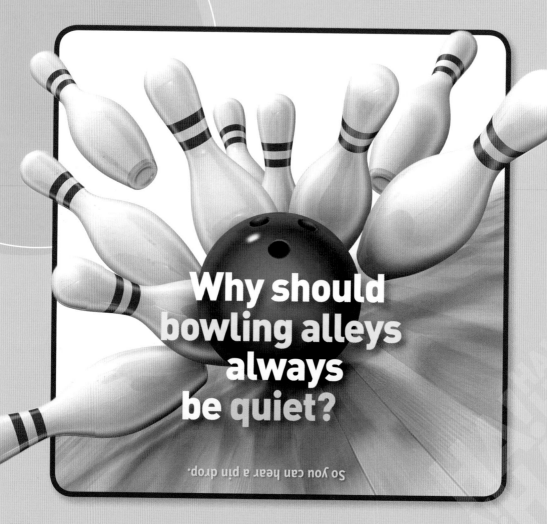

Why should bowling alleys always be quiet?

So you can hear a pin drop.

Q Why did the teacher wear sunglasses?

A Because her class was so bright.

Q What do you call a computer superhero?

A A screen saver.

Q Have you heard about the new restaurant on the moon?

A It's got great food but no atmosphere.

TONGUE TWISTER!

Say this fast three times:

Katie's kittens caught Kyle's kite.

173

Q What is a volcano?

A A mountain with hiccups.

Q What has 50 **heads** and 50 **tails?**

A A roll of pennies.

Q What do you give a dog with a fever?

A Mustard. It's the best thing for a hot dog!

Sound waves travel through a hippopotamus's jaws, allowing it to hear underwater.

KNOCK, KNOCK.

Who's there?
Zombies.
Zombies who?
Zombies make honey and zombies don't.

175

A gazillion gig gushed giving gophers

176

antic grapes gradually gooey guts.

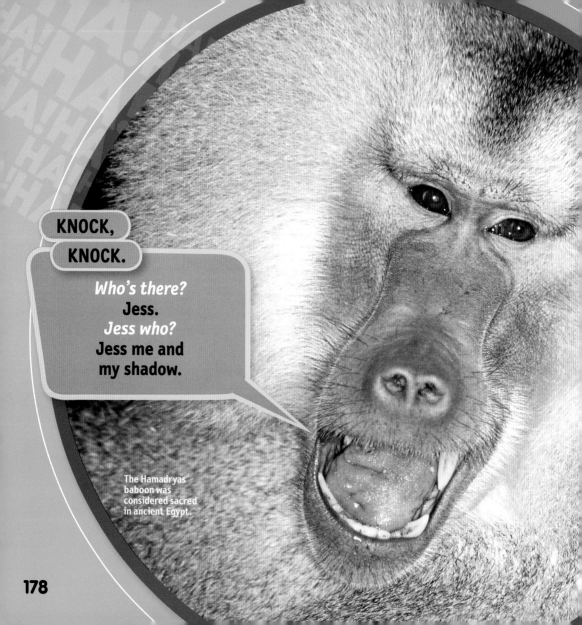

KNOCK, KNOCK.

Who's there?
Jess.
Jess who?
Jess me and my shadow.

The Hamadryas baboon was considered sacred in ancient Egypt.

Q

Why do magicians
do so well in school?

A

They're good at trick questions.

TONGUE
TWISTER!

Say this fast three times:

**A big black bug
bit a big black bear.**

Q How do you catch a squirrel?

A Climb a tree and act like a nut!

Say this fast three times:

Felix finds fresh french fries finer.

Q Why did the **computer** go to the orthodontist?

To improve its byte.

A

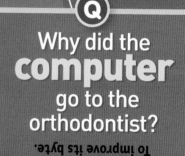

A parrot snake's fangs are located in the back of its mouth.

KNOCK, KNOCK.

Who's there?
Hutch.
Hutch who?
You'd better take care of that cold!

Macaws can live to be 65 years old.

183

Say this fast three times:

Crisp crusts crackle and crunch.

Q Why couldn't **anyone** find the deck of cards?

A They got lost in the shuffle.

Q Why didn't the duck doctor have any patients?

A Everyone knew he was a quack.

Q What did the bee say to the flower?

A "Hey, bud. When do you open?"

Q Why did the **traffic light** turn **red?**

A Wouldn't you if you had to change in the middle of the street?

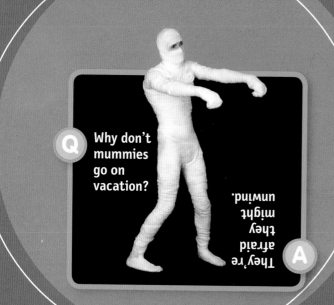

Q Why don't mummies go on vacation?

A They're afraid they might unwind.

Q What did one potato chip say to the other?

A "Shall we go for a dip?"

Young Amazon river dolphins are dark gray, but adults are solid pink or have pink blotches.

HA! HA! HA! HA! HA! HA! HA! HA! HA! HA! HA! HA!

186

What do you call

a fake noodle?

An impasta.

Polar bears have been spotted on sea ice hundreds of miles from shore.

KNOCK, KNOCK.

Who's there?
Eiffel.
Eiffel who?
Eiffel down
the steps.

Q What did the **eye-balls** say to each other?

A Just between the two of us, something smells!

A snail is robbed by four turtles. When he goes to the police, the officer asks, "Can you describe the turtles?"

The snail replies, "Not well. It all happened so fast."

Q What kind of **animal** would you **never** play **video games** with?

A A cheetah.

Q Where do **crayons** go on **vacation?**

A To a wax museum.

Q What do you get if you cross a **dinosaur** with a pig?

A Jurassic-pork.

Q Why was the man fired from the orange juice factory?

A Because he couldn't concentrate.

FATHER: How are your grades, son?

SON: Underwater, Dad.

FATHER: Underwater? What do you mean?

SON: They're below C level.

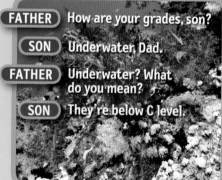

Q Where was the Declaration of Independence **signed?**

A At the bottom.

The ornate horned frog is sometimes called a Pac-Man frog—after the classic video game—because of its large mouth.

KNOCK, KNOCK.

Who's there?
Shirley.
Shirley who?
Shirley you know my name by now.

193

KNOCK, KNOCK.

Who's there?
Juicy.
Juicy who?
Juicy what I
just saw?

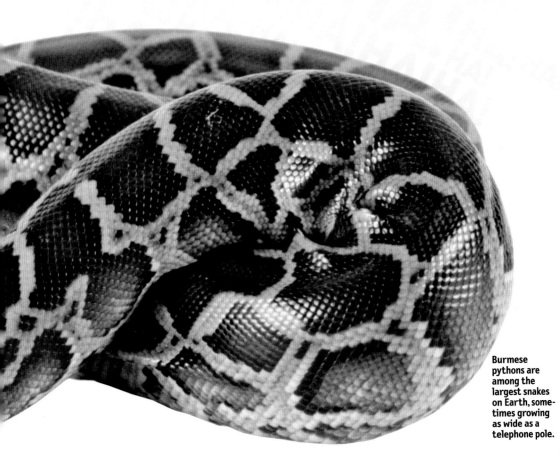

Burmese pythons are among the largest snakes on Earth, sometimes growing as wide as a telephone pole.

A mouse opossum's tail can be as long as the rest of its body.

KNOCK, KNOCK.

Who's there?
Meyer.
Meyer who?
Meyer nosy!

196

Say this fast three times:

Roscoe rescued Rosie from roaring rapids.

Q Why did the Pilgrims' pants keep falling down?

A Because their belt buckles were on their hats.

Q

What do you call a
pig
that does karate?

A

A pork chop.

Q

Why are giraffes so slow to apologize?

A

Because it takes them a long time to swallow their pride.

Q What does
lightning put on
during
rainy weather?

Thunderwear.

A

198

What do you call a rooster who wakes you up at the same time every morning?

An alarm cluck.

Adult male chickens are called roosters; young male chickens are called cockerels.

199

Orangutans find water to drink inside tree hollows, on wet leaves, or even on their own fur after a rain.

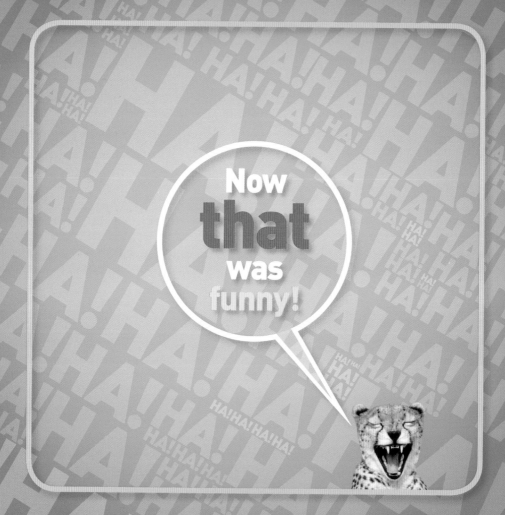

JOKEFINDER

203

Tongue twisters

ILLUSTRATIONCREDITS

Historical/GI; 100 (LO RT), Stephen Dalton/NHPA/Photoshot; 101, HPH Image Library/SS; 103 (LE), sabri deniz kizil/SS; 103 (RT), C./SS; 104, mountainpix/SS; 105 (UP), Eric Isselée/SS; 105 (LO), Anthony Berenyi/SS; 106 (LE), Andy Crawford/GI; 106 (RT), William Joseph Boch Photography/StockFood; 106 (RT inset), Joel Sartore/NationalGeographicStock.com; 107, Peter Zijlstra/SS; 108, Dariush M./SS; 109 (UP), Stephen Mcsween/SS; 109 (LO), Kasza/SS; 110-111, Corbis/SuperStock; 112 (UP), Gorilla/SS; 112 (LO), Myoko Komine/amana images/GI; 113, Tom & Pat Leeson; 114-115, CRWPitman/SS; 116, Foonia/SS; 117, James Laurie/SS; 118 (UP LE), Seregam/SS; 118 (UP RT), patti jean_images & designs by patti jean guerrero/SS; 118 (LO LE), Radu Razvan/SS; 118 (LO RT), Ryan Mcvay/GI; 119, topseller/SS; 120-121, Joel Sartore/National Geographic Creative; 122, Quayside/SS; 123 (LE), Digital Vision/GI; 123 (RT), Kurt De Bruyn/SS; 124 (UP), Digital Vision/GI; 124 (LO LE), Jeff Hunter/GI; 124 (LO RT), Dima Fadev/SS; 125, Stephen Coburn/SS; 126-127, Luis Francisco Cordero/SS; 128, Darrell Gulin/GI; 129 (UP), AnatolyM/SS; 129 (LO), Photodisc Green/GI; 130 (LE), Bill Losh/GI; 130 (UP RT), oksana2010/SS; 130 (LO RT), Svetlana Larina/SS; 131, Helen E. Grose/SS; 132-133, irink/SS; 134 (UP), Bambuh/SS; 135 (UP LE), Larry Lilac/Alamy; 135 (UP RT), Chris Hill/SS; 135 (LO), Danita Delimont/GI; 136 (LO), Rubberball Productions/GI; 137, B&T Media Group Inc./SS; 139 (CTR), Poznyakov/SS; 139 (CTR front), Dan Lee/SS; 140, Steven Hunt/The Image Bank/GI; 141 (UP LE), Michael Nichols/NationalGeographicStock.com; 141 (UP RT), Gerry Ellis/GI; 141 (LO LE), Terry Alexander/SS; 142 (LE), Comstock/Jupiterimages; 142 (UP RT), Spencer Jones/GI; 142 (LO RT), Eric Isselée/SS; 143, James Steidl/SS; 144-145, Jane Burton/naturepl.com; 146, BananaStock/Jupiterimages; 147, Eric Isselée/SS; 148, Brian Kenney; 149 (UP), Royalty-Free/Corbis; 149 (LO), Pavelk/SS; 150 (LO), Fuse/Corbis/GI; 151, Yakovleva Zinaida Vasilevna/SS; 152-153, Thomas Hoeffgen/GI; 154, Karl & Kay Amman/Photoshot; 155 (UP), foodanddrink-photos.com; 155 (LO), Kelly Redinger/Design Pics/Corbis; 156 (LE), Suzi Eszterhas/Minden Pictures; 156, hansenn/SS; 157, Fotopic/Index Stock Imagery, Inc./Photolibrary .com; 158-159, Luciano Candisani/Minden Pictures; 160 (background), Nicemonkey/SS; 160 (CTR), Jacob Hamblin/SS; 161 (UP LE), Imageman/SS; 161 (UP RT), NASA; 161 (LO), Paul Souders/GI; 162 (both), Eric Isselée/SS; 163, Ch'ien Lee/Minden Pictures; 164, Tatiana Morozova/SS; 166, David Courtenay/GI; 167, Tramont_ana/SS; 168-169, Armin Rose/SS; 170 (UP), Michael G Smith/SS; 170 (LO LE), Alexander Raths/SS; 170 (LO RT), Jiri Hera/SS; 171, Lucertolone/SS; 172, Solvod/SS; 173 (LE), Royalty-Free/Corbis; 173 (UP RT), AISPIX/SS; 173 (LO RT), bezmaski/SS; 174 (UP), James L. Amos/NationalGeographicStock.com; 174 (LO), BananaStock/Jupiterimages; 175, Gert Johannes Jacobus Vrey/SS; 176-177, Adisa/SS; 178, G. C. Kelley/Photo Researchers, Inc.; 179 (UP), G.K. & Vikki Hart/GI; 179 (LO), nialat/SS; 180 (LE), KV4000/SS; 180 (UP), Burke/Triolo/Brand X Pictures/PictureQuest; 181, Theo Allofs/zefa/Corbis/GI; 182-183, Vivid Pixels/SS; 184, Irina Rogova/SS; 185 (UP), Royalty-Free/Corbis; 185 (LO), manfredxy/SS; 186 (UP), pzAxe/SS; 186 (LO), AGphotographer/SS; 187, Kevin Schafer/Minden Pictures; 188, Sailorr/SS; 190, ZSSD/Minden Pictures; 191 (UP LE), Comstock/Jupiter Images; 191 (UP RT), Radius/SuperStock; 191 (LO RT), Image Source/GI; 192 (LE), Specta/SS; 192 (RT), Inga Nielsen/SS; 193, Zig Leszczynski/Animals Animals; 194-195, Jane Burton/naturepl.com; 196, Haroldo Palo Jr./NHPA/Photoshot; 197 (UP), Skip Brown/NationalGeographicStock.com; 197 (LO), Photodisc Green/GI; 198 (UP LE), akva/SS; 198 (UP RT), Anky/SS; 198 (LO), Jhaz Photography/SS; 199, Ursula/SS; 200, DLILLC/Corbis Documentary/VGC/GI

Published by National Geographic Partners, LLC. All rights reserved. Reproduction of the whole or any part of the contents without written permission from the publisher is prohibited.

Prepared by the Book Division
Nancy Laties Feresten, *Senior Vice President, Editor in Chief, Children's Books*
Jonathan Halling, *Design Director, Books and Children's Publishing*
Jay Sumner, *Director of Photography, Children's Publishing*
Jennifer Emmett, *Editorial Director, Children's Books*
Carl Mehler, *Director of Maps*
R. Gary Colbert, *Production Director*
Jennifer A. Thornton, *Managing Editor*

Based on the "Just Joking" department in
***National Geographic Kids* magazine**
Kelley Miller, *Senior Photo Editor*
Julide Dengel, *Designer*
Margaret Krauss, *Researcher*

Staff for This Book
Robin Terry, *Project Editor*
Eva Absher, *Managing Art Director*
Kelley Miller, *Illustrations Editor*
David M. Seager, *Art Director/Designer*
Grace Hill, *Associate Managing Editor*
Joan Gossett, *Production Editor*
Lewis R. Bassford, *Production Manager*
Susan Borke, *Legal and Business Affairs*
Kate Olesin, *Assistant Editor*
Kathryn Robbins, *Design Production Assistant*
Hillary Moloney, *Illustrations Assistant*
Jean Mendoza, Catherine Monson, *Editorial Interns*

Manufacturing and Quality Management
Christopher A. Liedel, *Chief Financial Officer*
Phillip L. Schlosser, *Senior Vice President*
Chris Brown, *Technical Director*
Nicole Elliott, *Manager*
Rachel Faulise, *Manager*
Robert L. Barr, *Manager*

Since 1888, the National Geographic Society has funded more than 12,000 research, exploration, and preservation projects around the world. The Society receives funds from National Geographic Partners, LLC, funded in part by your purchase. A portion of the proceeds from this book supports this vital work. To learn more, visit natgeo.com/info.

NATIONAL GEOGRAPHIC and Yellow Border Design are trademarks of the National Geographic Society, used under license.

For more information, please visit nationalgeographic.com, call 1-800-647-5463, or write to the following address:
National Geographic Partners
1145 17th Street N.W.
Washington, D.C. 20036-4688 U.S.A.

Visit us online at nationalgeographic.com/books

For librarians and teachers: ngchildrensbooks.org

More for kids from National Geographic: natgeokidsbooks.co.uk

For information about special discounts for bulk purchases, please contact National Geographic Books Special Sales: specialsales@natgeo.com

For rights or permissions inquiries, please contact National Geographic Books Subsidiary Rights: bookrights@natgeo.com

Library of Congress Cataloging-in-Publication Data

Just joking: 300 hilarious jokes, tricky tongue twisters, and ridiculous riddles/by National Geographic kids.
p. cm.
ISBN 978-1-4263-0930-4 (pbk. : alk. paper)—ISBN 978-1-4263-0944-1 (library binding : alk. paper)
1. Wit and humor, Juvenile. I. National Geographic Society (U.S.)
PN6166.J87 2012
818′.602—dc22

2011034649

2018 Aldi edition ISBN: 978-1-4263-3406-1

Printed in China